CROCK POT CHICKEN RECIPES

+60 Quick & Easy Recipes and Dishes to Stay Healthy, and Find Your Well-Being

CROCK POT CHICKEN RECIPES 1

INTRODUCTION 5
Artichoke Chicken and Rice 7
Asian Flavors Slow Cooked Chicken 9
Barbecue Chicken Tenders 11
Barbecued Chicken for Sandwiches 13
Betty's Garlic Chicken with Cabbage 15
Bev's Italian Chicken 17
Beverly's Creamy Broccoli Chicken 19
Beverly's Healthy Crockpot Chicken Creole 21
Brown Rice and Chicken 23
Cheese and Chile Stuffed Chicken Breasts 25
Cheesy Artichoke Chicken With Pasta 27
Chicken & Apple-Pecan Stuffing 29
Chicken & Artichoke Casserole 31
Chicken & Asparagus in Onion Sauce 33
Chicken & Broccoli Casserole 35
Chicken & Cornmeal Dumplings 38
Chicken & Vegetable Pasta Sauce 40
Chicken a la King 42
Chicken and Black Beans 44
Chicken and Cheddar Sauce 46
Chicken and Corn Chowder 48
Chicken and Dressing, Slow Cooker 50
Chicken And Green Onion Curry 52
Chicken and Mushrooms 54
Chicken and Olives 56
Chicken and Rice in an Oven Cooking Bag 58
Chicken and Rice Parmesan 60
Chicken and Sausage 62
Chicken and Shrimp 64
Chicken and Stuffing 66
Chicken Breasts in Creamy Creole Sauce 68
Chicken Burritos 70
Chicken Cacciatore 72
Chicken Cassoulet With Navy Beans 74
Chicken Chili with Hominy 76
Chicken Chow Mein 78
Chicken Cordon Bleu Recipe, Slow Cooker 81
Chicken Delish 83
Chicken Divan with Broccoli and Noodles 85
Chicken Enchiladas for the Slow Cooker 87
Chicken Las Vegas 89

Chicken Lasagna	91
Chicken Marengo	94
Chicken Parisienne	96
Chicken Parmesan	98
Chicken Ragout	100
Chicken Reuben Casserole	102
Chicken Rice Casserole with Green Beans	104
Chicken Thighs, Tex-Mex Style	106
Chicken with Artichokes	108
Chicken with Bacon and Macaroni	110
Chicken With Bacon and Wine	112
Chicken With Biscuits	114
Chicken with Cranberries	116
Chicken with Dried Beef	118
Chicken With Garlic and Pineapple	120
Chicken with Grapes	122
Chicken With Honey	124
Chicken with Macaroni and Smoked Gouda Cheese	126
Chicken With Noodles, Slow Cooker	128
Chicken with Onions	131
Chicken With Parsley Dumplings	133
Chicken With Pearl Onions and Mushrooms	135
CONCLUSION	137

INTRODUCTION

Chicken is one of the most versatile ingredients when it comes to the family of meats. Healthy and tasty, you can add it to almost any lunch or dinner dish that you can think of to make it a truly well-rounded meal. Indeed, chicken appears in almost every popular cuisine of the many cultures around the world, and if it is not in the main dish of that country, then it certainly has a place somewhere in day-to-day gastronomy. Yet due to the fact that it is such a widely used meat, there are

some individuals and families who might grow bored with having to prepare it for so many meals per night. They feel they have prepared almost every dish they can think of, or they do not know where to find other more innovative recipes to keep the meals fresh and new.
Crock Pot Chicken Recipes is the solution to that problem of the humdrum dinner.
Not only are there a handful of delicious meals that are easy to follow and come out wonderful, but these are also recipes that rely on one of the most helpful pieces of equipment a kitchen can feature: a crockpot. With this tool, you simply load it up with the ingredients that you need for the dish, turn the heat and timer settings to where they need to be according to your recipes, and walk away.

There's not much more to it! You can delight your family and your friends with these scrumptious recipes that will have them thinking you slaved in the kitchen for hours on end! When in reality, all you did was load your crockpot and have the foresight to prepare yourself with these exquisite meal ideas.

Artichoke Chicken and Rice

INGREDIENTS

- 1 to 1 1/2 pounds chicken breasts halves
- 1/4 cup flour
- 3 tablespoons Parmesan cheese
- 1 teaspoon salt
- 1/2 teaspoon coarsely ground pepper
- 1 teaspoon paprika
- 2 tablespoons olive oil
- 1 1/2 cups converted rice
- 1/4 cup chopped red bell pepper or pimiento
- 4 green onions, chopped
- 4 ounces mushrooms, sliced
- 1 1/2 cups chicken broth (use bouillon, canned, or base)
- 1 can cream of celery soup, low fat
- 1 can artichokes, quartered and drained

PREPARATION

1. In a large skillet over medium heat, heat the olive oil.
2. Combine flour, cheese, salt, pepper, and paprika.
3. Dredge chicken in the flour mixture then brown in the hot oil.
4. Transfer chicken to the slow cooker. In the hot skillet, saute bell pepper, green onions, and mushrooms for about 2 minutes; add chicken broth and soup, stirring to combine thoroughly; pour over chicken. Stir in rice and artichokes; cover and cook for 5 to 6 hours on low.

Asian Flavors Slow Cooked Chicken

INGREDIENTS

- 3 lb. chicken thighs or leg quarters
- 1/4 cup Hoisin sauce
- 1/4 cup plum sauce
- 1/4 cup low sodium soy sauce
- 1 medium piece fresh ginger root, about 2 inches, peeled and thinly sliced or grated
- juice of 1 whole fresh lime
- 3 tbsp. corn starch

PREPARATION

1. Remove skin from chicken, if desired. Combine hoisin sauce, plum sauce, soy sauce, ginger, lime, and cornstarch in a large bowl or food storage bag; blend well.
2. Add the chicken pieces, turning to coat well. Put the chicken and marinade in the slow cooker.
3. Cover and cook on LOW for 5 to 7 hours, until chicken is tender and juices run clear. Serve with hot cooked rice.
4. Serves 4.

Barbecue Chicken Tenders

INGREDIENTS

• 1 to 1 1/2 pound chicken tenders • 3/4 cup ketchup • 1 teaspoon liquid
smoke • 1 teaspoon soy sauce • 1 tablespoon margarine • 2 tablespoons
brown sugar • 1 teaspoon mustard • 1 green bell pepper, chopped • 1
onion, chopped • split sandwich buns, warm or toasted or hot cooked rice

PREPARATION

1. Combine chicken tenders, ketchup, liquid smoke, soy sauce, margarine,
brown sugar, mustard, bell pepper and onion in the slow cooker or crockpot.
2. Cover and cook on low for 6 to 7 hours.
3. Serve chicken tenders on sandwich buns or serve with hot cooked rice.
4. Serves 6.

Barbecued Chicken for Sandwiches

INGREDIENTS

• 4 lb. fryer chicken • 1 1/2 to 2 c. hickory smoke flavored barbecue sauce
• 8 to 10 fresh buns

PREPARATION

1. Boil the chicken until cooked and tender.
2. After it cools, pull meat from bones and put in a slow cooker or Crock Pot.
3. Cover with sauce. Cook on high for 3 to 5 hours, stirring every 30 minutes.
4. Chicken will shred during stirring.
5. Serve on buns.
6. Serves 8 to 10.

Betty's Garlic Chicken with Cabbage

INGREDIENTS

• 1 whole chicken • 1 medium onion chopped • 3-8 garlic cloves or use
garlic salt or garlic powder to you liking • salt and pepper to taste • 1 head
cabbage • 2 tablespoons butter • pepper

PREPARATION

1. Season chicken and place in slow cooker/Crock Pot. Add onion and garlice
cloves and salt and pepper. Fill slow cooker/Crock Pot 1/4-way with water,
cover and cook on HIGH for 4 to 5 hours. The chicken should be tender and
falling off of the bone.
2. During the last hour of cooking the chicken, cut up 1 head of green
cabbage, core removed. Place cabbage in a large pot with a shallow amount of
water -- about 1/2-to 1 cup.
3. Add two tablespoons of butter and sprinkle generously with garlic salt and
pepper. Cover and cook on medium high heat for 20 to 30 minutes, until tender;
drain.
4. When chicken and cabbage are done, place some cabbage in a bowl and

top with chicken and some of the chicken broth. You can adjust any of the
seasonings and the butter.

Bev's Italian Chicken

INGREDIENTS

- 6 to 8 frozen boneless chicken breast halves • 1 envelope French's Brand
Italian Spaghetti Sauce - dry mix • 1 can (14.5 ounces) diced tomatoes • 1
small can (8 ounces) tomato sauce • Parmesan Cheese

PREPARATION

1. Place the chicken in the crock. Sprinkle the dry mix spaghetti sauce over
top. Add the can of tomatoes and the can of tomato sauce. Cook all day [7 to 9
hours] on LOW or 1/2 Day [3 1/2 to 4 1/2 hours] on HIGH.
2. Serve with Penne pasta and top with Parmesan Cheese.
3. posted by Beverly

Beverly's Creamy Broccoli Chicken

INGREDIENTS

- 1 can (approx. 10 1/2 ounces) condensed Cream of Broccoli Soup
- boneless chicken breasts (as many as you need) - I buy the frozen ones with
6-7 in a bag - approx. 3 pounds • 1 bag (12 to 16 ounces) frozen broccoli
- salt and pepper • 1 cup milk

PREPARATION

1. Place chicken pieces in the crock pot. Cover with the frozen broccoli and
spoon the cream of broccoli soup over all. Add salt and pepper to taste.
2. Cover and cook on LOW 6 to 8 hours or on HIGH 3 to 4 hours. (Boneless
chicken breasts might be dry if cooked too long.) Add milk about 45 minutes
before done, or 30 minutes if cooking on high.
3. Serve poured over rice!!! Yummy!

Beverly's Healthy Crockpot Chicken Creole

INGREDIENTS

- 2 1/2 to 3 lbs. chicken thighs or breasts, skin removed • 1 cup chopped
celery • 1 red bell pepper, sliced • 1 green bell pepper, sliced • 1 medium onion, sliced • 1 can (4 ounces) sliced mushrooms • 1 can (14.5
ounces) tomatoes • 1 teaspoon garlic powder • 3 packages sugar substitute
- 1 teaspoon Creole or Cajun seasoning blend • 1/2 teaspoon ground
paprika • salt and pepper to taste • Louisiana hot sauce or Tabasco, to taste
- 2 hot cooked rice

PREPARATION

1. Place chicken in bottom of crockpot. Combine remaining ingredients,
except rice, and add to crockpot. Cook on HIGH 4 to 5 hours or on LOW for 7 to
8 hours. Spoon Creole chicken mixture over hot cooked rice.
2. Serves 4 to 6.

Brown Rice and Chicken

INGREDIENTS

- 1 1/2 cups diced cooked chicken • 1/2 cup chopped onion • 2 stalks
celery, chopped • 2 c. cooked brown rice • 1/4 c. dry white wine • 2 c.
chicken broth • 1/2 cup sliced or slivered almonds • toasted sliced or
slivered almonds• for topping, optional

PREPARATION

1. Combine all ingredients in slow cooker. Cook on low 6 to 8 hours or on
automatic 4 to 5 hours. Tope with toasted sliced almonds, if desired.
2. •To toast nuts, spread out in a single layer on a baking sheet. Toast in a
350° oven, stirring occasionally, for 10 to 15 minutes. Or, toast in an ungreased
skillet over medium heat, stirring, until golden brown and aromatic.

Cheese and Chile Stuffed Chicken Breasts

INGREDIENTS

- 4 boneless, skinned chicken breast halves, pounded thin • 3 ounces
cream cheese • 3/4 cups shredded Cheddar or Monterey Jack cheese • 4
ounces green chiles • 1/2 teaspoon chili powder • salt and pepper to taste
- 1 can cream of mushroom soup • 1/2 cup hot enchilada sauce

PREPARATION

1. Combine cream cheese, shredded cheese, chiles, chili powder and salt and
pepper. Place a generous dollop on each flattened chicken breast, then roll up.
Place chicken rolls in the slow cooker/Crock Pot, seam-side down. Top chicken
breast rolls with remaining cheese mixture, soup, and enchilada sauce. Cover
and cook on LOW for 6 to 7 hours. Recipe by Southernfood.about.com.
2. Serves 4.

Cheesy Artichoke Chicken With Pasta

INGREDIENTS

- 1 to 1 1/2 lbs boneless chicken breast tenders, rinsed, dried, and cubed or
use cubed boneless chicken breast • 4 to 6 oz roasted red peppers, chopped
- 1 can (15oz) artichoke hearts, quartered • 8 oz process American cheese
- 2 teaspoons Worcestershire sauce • 1 can (10oz) 98% fat free cream of
mushroom soup (or other cream of.. soup) • 2 cups shredded cheddar cheese
- 4 cups hot cooked pasta (8 to 10 oz) • salt & pepper to taste

PREPARATION

1. In a 3 1/2-quart or larger Crock Pot combine chicken, peppers, artichokes,
American cheese, Worcestershire sauce, and soup in the slow cooker/Crock Pot.
Cover and cook on low for 6 to 8 hours. About 15 minutes before serving, add
shredded Cheddar cheese and hot cooked pasta. Taste and add salt and pepper as
needed.
2. Serves 4 to 6.

Chicken & Apple-Pecan Stuffing

INGREDIENTS

• 4 to 6 boneless, skinless chicken breasts • 3 tablespoons butter • 1/2
cup chopped onion • 1/2 cup chopped celery • 1 cup chopped apple (about
1 apple) • 1/3 cup applesauce • 1/4 cup chopped pecans • 1 box Stove
Top stuffing mix (6 oz) • 1/2 cup water • 1 can cream of chicken soup
(Healthy Request or low fat)

PREPARATION

1. Wash chicken breasts and pat dry; place in Crock Pot. Melt the butter in a
skillet over medium low heat and saute the chopped onion, celery, and apple.
Add pecans, water, applesauce, cream of chicken soup, and stuffing mix. Mix
together; spoon over chicken in the Crock Pot. Cover and cook on low for 6 to 8
hours.
2. Serves 4.

Chicken & Artichoke Casserole

INGREDIENTS

- 3 to 4 pounds chicken pieces • salt and pepper • 1/2 teaspoon paprika
- 1 to 2 tablespoons butter • 1 teaspoon chicken bouillon granules or equivalent base, dissolved in 1/2 cup hot water • 3 tablespoons dry white wine or sherry • 1/2 teaspoon dried tarragon • 1/4 pound mushrooms, sliced • 1 tablespoon cornstarch blended with 1 tablespoon cold water • 1 can (15 ounces) artichoke hearts, drained

PREPARATION

1. Wash chicken and pat dry. Season with salt and pepper and paprika. In a large skillet, brown chicken in about half of the butter. Transfer to slow cooker.
Pour broth and wine into skillet. Stir to loosen brown bits. Pour over chicken then season with tarragon. Cover and cook on LOW for 6 to 8 hours. Just before serving, saute mushrooms in remaining butter until tender and browned. Turn slow cooker to high.
2. When sauce is hot and simmering, stir in cornstarch and water mixture.

Cook until thickened. Add sauteed mushrooms and artichoke hearts; heat
through and serve.3. Serves 4.

Chicken & Asparagus in Onion Sauce

INGREDIENTS

- 4 to 6 chicken breasts • 1/2 cup chicken broth • 1 can (10 1/2 ounces)
condensed cream of onion soup • 1/4 to 1/2 teaspoon tarragon, if desired
- 1 teaspoon lemon and herb seasoning • salt and pepper to taste • 1
bunch asparagus, or 10 ounce package frozen , thawed

PREPARATION

1. Combine all ingredients except asparagus; cover and cook on low for 6 to 8
hours. Add asparagus and cook on high an additional 20 to 30 minutes, or until
asparagus is tender. Thicken sauce with a mixture of 1 to 2 tablespoons of
cornstarch and a little cold water if desired. Serve over rice or noodles.
2. Serves 4 to 6.

Chicken & Broccoli Casserole

INGREDIENTS

- 4 c. cubed cooked chicken or turkey • 1 (4 oz.) can sliced mushrooms,
drained, or use fresh mushrooms • 1 (5 oz.) can sliced water chestnuts • 1
(10 to 12 oz.) pkg. frozen chopped broccoli, about 1 1/2 to 2 cups • 1/2 cup
chopped onion • 1 cup Sauce (below) • Paprika • .
- Sauce: • 1/4 c. butter • 1/4 c. flour • 1/2 tsp. salt • 1/4 tsp. pepper • 1 c. chicken broth • 1/2 cup evaporated milk • 2 tbsp. cooking
sherry

PREPARATION

1. Spread half the chicken in the slow cooker or Crock Pot. Top with the
mushrooms, water chestnuts, onion and broccoli. Arrange remaining chicken on
top. Cover with sauce (directions below). Sprinkle with paprika. Cover and cook
on low for 4 to 6 hours or high for 2 to 3 hours, or until chicken is thoroughly
cooked.
2. Sauce Instructions: Melt butter in medium saucepan over low heat. Blend
in flour, salt, and pepper.

3. Cook over low heat, stirring until mixture is smooth and bubbly. Remove
from heat. Stir in broth and milk. Heat to boiling, stirring constantly. Boil and
stir 1 minute. Remove from heat; stir in wine. Makes about 2 cups.

Chicken & Cornmeal Dumplings

INGREDIENTS

- 2 cups diced potatoes • 1 1/2 cups chicken broth • 1 (12 oz.) can V-8
or tomato juice (1 1/2 cups) • 1/2 cup sliced celery • 1/2 cup chopped
onion • 1/2 tsp. salt • 1 tsp. chili powder • 4 to 6 drops Tabasco sauce
- 2 cups cubed, cooked chicken • 1 1/2 to 2 cups frozen cut green beans,
thawed • 1 1/4 cups packaged biscuit mix • 1/3 cup yellow cornmeal • 2
tbsp. finely chopped fresh parsley or snipped fresh chives • 1 cup shredded
Cheddar cheese • 2/3 cup milk

PREPARATION

1. Combine potatoes, chicken broth, vegetable juice, celery, onion, chili
powder, salt and hot pepper sauce in the slow cooker. Cover and cook on LOW
for 4 hours. Turn to HIGH and heat until bubbly; add thawed green beans and
cubed chicken. In a mixing bowl, combine biscuit mix, cornmeal, 1/2 cup of the
shredded cheese and parsley or chives. Add milk and stir until just moistened.
Drop by tablespoons onto stew; cover.

2. Cook 2 hours and 30 minutes longer, without lifting the cover. Sprinkle
dumplings with the remaining shredded cheese 5 minutes before done. Serves 4.

Chicken & Vegetable Pasta Sauce

INGREDIENTS

- 1 to 1 1/2 lbs chicken tenders, cubed (or use boneless chicken breasts)
- 2 medium onions, coarsely chopped
- 1 medium (or 2 small) zucchini, quartered and sliced 1/2-inch thick
- 1 green bell pepper, coarsely chopped
- 2 to 3 cloves garlic, chopped or thinly sliced
- 1 can (28 oz) crushed tomatoes
- 1 can (15 oz) diced tomatoes
- 1 package country gravy mix (or chicken gravy mix)
- 1/2 teaspoon dry sweet basil
- 1 teaspoon dry leaf oregano

PREPARATION

1. Combine all ingredients in the slow cooker/Crock Pot (3 1/2-quart or larger).
2. Cover and cook on low for 6 to 9 hours.
3. Serve over hot cooked pasta or as a sauce for lasagna.
4. Serves 6 to 8.

Chicken a la King

INGREDIENTS

- 3 to 4 cups cooked chicken or turkey, diced • 1/2 cup green pepper,
finely chopped • 1/4 cup onion, finely chopped • 1/2 cup celery, finely
chopped • 1 jar (2 ounces) chopped pimento (or chopped red bell pepper)
- 1 can (4 ounces) sliced mushrooms, drained • 2 cans (10 3/4 ounces)
condensed cream of chicken soup (or cream of mushroom) • 1 pkg. (10
oz.) frozen peas, about 1 1/2 cups

PREPARATION

1. Combine all ingredients except peas in the slow cooker. Stir gently to mix.
2. Cover and cook on low 5 to 7 hours. Turn to high and add peas about 45
minutes before serving.
3. Serves 4.

Chicken and Black Beans

INGREDIENTS

- 3 to 4 boneless chicken breast halves, cut in strips • 1 can (12 to 15 ounces) corn, drained • 1 can (15 oz) black beans, rinsed and drained • 2 teaspoons gound cumin • 2 teaspoons chili powder • 1 onion, halved and thinly sliced • 1 green bell pepper, cut in strips • 1 can (14.5 ounces) diced tomatoes • 1 can (6 ounces) tomato paste

PREPARATION

1. Combine all ingredients in slow cooker. Cover and cook on low for 5 to 6 hours.
2. Garnish with shredded cheese, if desired. Serve fiesta chicken and black beans with warmed flour tortillas, or over rice.
3. Serves 4.

Chicken and Cheddar Sauce

INGREDIENTS

- 2 pounds chicken pieces, skin removed • 2 tablespoons butter
- 1/2 cup ham strips • 10 3/4 ounces condensed Cheddar cheese soup • 1 tomato, chopped • 1 cup chopped onions • 1/4 teaspoon dried sweet basil

PREPARATION

1. Brown chicken in butter; transfer to slow cooker. Brown ham and place on chicken. Combine remaining ingredients; pour over chicken and ham. Cover and cook on low 7 to 9 hours, or until chicken is tender.

Chicken and Corn Chowder

INGREDIENTS

- 1 can (10 3/4 ounces) cream of potato soup • 1 can (10 3/4 ounces)
cream of chicken soup • 1 cup diced chicken or about 2 cans (4 to 6 ounces
each) chunk chicken • 1 can (12 to 15 ounces) whole kernel corn, drained
- 1 cup chicken stock or broth • 1/4 cup diced red bell pepper or roasted
red bell pepper • 1 can chopped mild green chile • 1/2 teaspoon salt
- 1/8 teaspoon black pepper • 1/4 teaspoon dried leaf thyme • 1 cup
milk

PREPARATION

1. Combine the soups, chicken, corn, chicken broth, bell pepper and chile,
salt, pepper, and thyme in a 4-to 6-quart crockpot.
2. Cover and cook on LOW for 4 to 5 hours.
3. Add milk and cook for about 30 minutes longer, or until hot.
4. Serves 4 to 6.

Chicken and Dressing, Slow Cooker

INGREDIENTS

- 1 bag seasoned stuffing mix, 14 to 16 ounces • 3 to 4 cups cooked diced
chicken • 3 cans cream of chicken soup • 1/2 cup milk • 1 to 2 cups
mild cheddar cheese, shredded

PREPARATION

1. Prepare stuffing mix according to package directions and place in 5
quart Crock Pot. Stir in 2 cans of Cream of Chicken soup. In a mixing bowl, stir
together cubed chicken, 1 can cream of chicken soup and milk. Spread over
stuffing in slow cooker. Sprinkle cheese over top. Cover and cook on Low for 4
to 6 hour or on High for 2 to 3 hours.
2. Serves 6 to 8.

Chicken And Green Onion Curry

INGREDIENTS

- 1 medium onion, thinly sliced
- 3 medium cloves garlic, minced or pressed
- 1 tablespoon fresh ginger root, grated
- 1 cinnamon stick
- 1/2 teaspoon ground cumin
- 1/2 teaspoon crushed red pepper flakes
- 1 teaspoon curry powder
- 1/2 teaspoon ground turmeric
- dash ground cloves
- 1/4 teaspoon ground cardamom
- 3 1/2 pounds chicken pieces, skin removed
- 1/2 cup chicken broth
- 2 tablespoons cornstarch, blended with
- 2 tablespoons cold water
- salt
- chopped fresh cilantro, for garnish
- 1/4 to 1/2 cup green onions, with tops, sliced

PREPARATION

1. In a medium to large slow cooker, combine the thinly sliced onion, garlic, cinnamon, ginger, cumin, red pepper flakes, turmeric, cloves, and cardamom.
2. Arrange the chicken pieces over onion mixture. Pour broth over chicken.

Cover and cook on LOW setting until the chicken is very tender and juices run
clear when pierced, about 6 to 7 hours.
3. Gently lift chicken to a warm serving dish and keep warm.
4. Skim and discard fat from cooking liquid, if necessary; remove and discard
cinnamon stick.
5. Mix cornstarch with cold water; blend into cooking liquid.
6. Increase cooker heat setting to high; cover and cook, stirring 2 or 3 times,
until sauce thickens.
7. Add salt to taste, and the sauce over the chicken.
8. Garnish with cilantro and sliced green onions.

Chicken and Mushrooms

INGREDIENTS

- 6 chicken breast halves, bone-in, skin removed • 1 1/4 tsp. salt • 1/4
tsp. pepper • 1/4 tsp. paprika • 2 teaspoons chicken bouillon granules
- 1 1/2 cup sliced mushrooms • 1/2 cup sliced green onions • 1/2 cup
dry white wine • 2/3 cup evaporated milk • 5 tsp. cornstarch • Minced
fresh parsley • hot cooked rice

PREPARATION

1. In a small bowl, mix salt, pepper and paprika. Rub all of the mixture into
the chicken.
2. In a slow cooker, alternate layers of chicken, bouillon granules,
mushrooms, and green onions. Pour wine over top. DO NOT STIR.
3. Cover and cook on HIGH for 2 1/2 to 3 hours or on LOW for 5 to 6 hours,
or until chicken is tender but not falling off bone. Baste one about halfway
through cooking if possible.
4. Remove chicken and vegetables to a platter with a slotted spoon.
5. Cover with foil and keep warm.

6. In a small saucepan, combine evaporated milk and cornstarch until smooth.
Gradually stir in 2 cups of the cooking liquid. Stirring over medium heat, bring
to a boil and boil for 1 to 2 minutes, or until thickened.
7. Spoon some of the sauce over chicken and garnish with minced parsley.
Serve remaining sauce on the side.
8. Serve with hot cooked rice.

Chicken and Olives

INGREDIENTS

- 3 to 3 1/2 pounds chicken pieces • 1 clove garlic, minced • 1 lg. onion, chopped • 2 bay leaves • 3/4 c. beer • 8 oz. tomato sauce • 1/2 c. pimento stuffed olives

PREPARATION

1. Wash chicken pieces and pat dry; season with salt and pepper. Combine all remaining ingredients, except chicken; stir well. Add chicken, stirring to coat well, make sure all chicken is coated. Cover and cook on low for 7 to 9 hours.
2. Serves 4 to 6.

Chicken and Rice in an Oven Cooking Bag

INGREDIENTS

- 3 pounds chicken parts • 2/3 cup water • 1 cup raw converted rice
- 1 package dry onion soup mix • 1 can cream of chicken soup or cream of
chicken soup with herbs

PREPARATION

1. Rinse chicken and pat dry. Set aside. Combine rice, soup, and water in
Crock Pot; stir well to mix in soup. Place chicken in a roasting bag; add dry
onion soup mix. Shake bag to coat chicken well. Puncture 4 to 6 holes in bottom
of bag. Fold top of bag over chicken and place in Crock Pot on top of rice. Cover
and cook on LOW for 6 to 8 hours, until chicken is tender and rice is done but
not mushy.

Chicken and Rice Parmesan

INGREDIENTS

- 1 envelope onion soup mix
- 1 can (10 3/4 ounces) condensed cream of mushroom soup, reduced fat
- 1 can (10 3/4 ounces) condensed cream of chicken soup, reduced fat
- 1 1/2 cups low or no fat milk
- 1 cup dry white wine
- 1 cup white rice
- 6 boneless chicken breast halves, without skin
- 2 tablespoons butter
- 2/3 cup grated Parmesan cheese

PREPARATION

1. Mix onion soup, condensed cream soups, milk, wine and rice. Spray Crock Pot w/pam. Lay chicken breasts in Crock Pot, top with 1 teaspoon of butter, pour soup mixture over all, then sprinkle with the Parmesan cheese. Cook on low 8 to 10 hours or on high for 4 to 6 hours.
2. Serves 6.

Chicken and Sausage

INGREDIENTS

• 3 carrots, cut in 1/2 inch slices • 1/2 cup chopped onion • 1/2 cup
water • 1 (6 oz.) can tomato paste • 1/2 cup dry red wine • 1 teaspoon garlic powder • 1/2 teaspoon dried thyme, crushed • 1/8 teaspoon
ground cloves • 1 bay leaf • 2 (15 oz.) cans navy beans, drained • 4
boneless skinless chicken breast halves • 1/2 lb. fully cooked Polish sausage
or other smoked sausage, sliced 1/4-inch thick

PREPARATION

1. In small saucepan, bring carrots, onions, and water to a boil. Simmer
covered 5 minutes. Transfer to 3 1/2 to 4 quart crock pot. Stir in tomato paste,
wine, and seasonings; add beans. Place chicken on top of bean mixture. Place
sausage on top of chicken. Cover. Cook on low heat setting for 6 to 8 hours or
high heat for 3 to 4 hours. Before serving, remove bay leaves and skim off fat.
2. Serve as a stew or with hot cooked rice.
3. 4 to 6 servings.

Chicken and Shrimp

INGREDIENTS

- 2 pounds chicken, boneless thighs and breasts, skin removed, cut in chunks
- 2 tablespoons of extra virgin olive oil
- 1 cup chopped onion
- 2 cloves garlic, minced
- 1/4 cup parsley, minced
- 1/2 cup white wine
- 1 large can (15 ounces) tomato sauce
- 1 teaspoon dried leaf basil
- 1 pound uncooked shrimp, peeled and deveined
- salt and freshly ground black pepper, to taste
- 1 pound fettuccine, linguine, or spaghetti

PREPARATION

1. In a large skillet or sauté pan over medium heat, heat the olive oil. Add the chicken chunks and cook, stirring, until lightly browned. Remove chicken to slow cooker.
2. Add a little more oil to the pan and sauté the onion, garlic, and parsley for about 1 minute. Remove from heat and stir in the wine, tomato sauce, and dried basil. Pour the mixture over chicken in slow cooker.
3. Cover and cook on LOW for 4 to 5 hours.
4. Stir in shrimp, cover, and cook on LOW for about 1 hour longer.

5. Season with salt and freshly ground black pepper, to taste.
6. Just before the dish is done, cook the pasta in boiling salted water as
directed on the package.

Chicken and Stuffing

INGREDIENTS

- 4 boneless chicken breast halves, without skin • 4 slices Swiss cheese
- 1 can (10 1/2 ounce) condensed cream of chicken soup • 1 can (10 1/2 ounce) condensed cream of mushroom soup • 1 cup chicken broth • 1/4 cup milk • 2 to 3 cups Pepperidge Farm Herb Stuffing Mix or Homemade Stuffing Mix • 1/2 cup melted butter •See Sandy's Notes • salt and pepper to taste

PREPARATION

1. Season chicken breasts with salt and pepper; place chicken breasts slow cooker.
2. Pour chicken broth over chicken breasts.
3. Put one slice of Swiss cheese on each breast.
4. Combine both cans of soup and milk. Cover chicken breasts with soup mixture.
5. Sprinkle stuffing mix over all. Drizzle melted butter on top.
6. Cook on low for 6-8 hours.

•Notes: You can also mix the chicken broth with the soup and you get almost the same results.

If you pour the broth over the chicken it keeps the chicken moist and tender. •I
only used 1/2 the amount of butter called for, and would use more with another
cup of stuffing mix next time.

Chicken Breasts in Creamy Creole Sauce

INGREDIENTS

- 1 bunch green onions (6 to 8, with most of the green part) • 2 slices
bacon • 1 teaspoon Creole or Cajun seasoning • 3 tablespoons butter • 4
tablespoons flour • 3/4 cup chicken broth • 1 to 2 tablespoons tomato paste
- 4 boneless chicken breast halves • 1/4 to 1/2 cup half and half or milk

PREPARATION

1. In a saucepan, melt butter over medium low heat. Add onions and bacon,
cook and stir for 2 minutes. Add flour, stir and cook for 2 more minutes. Add
chicken broth; cook until thick then add tomato paste. Place chicken breasts in
the slow cooker/Crock Pot; add sauce mixture. Cover and cook on low for 6 to 7
hours, stirring after 3 hours. Stir in milk about 20 to 30 minutes before done.
Serve over pasta or rice.
2. Serves 4.

Chicken Burritos

INGREDIENTS

- 2 cups chopped cooked chicken • 1 packet (1 ounce) burrito seasoning
mix • 1 can (16 ounces) refried beans • 6 flour tortillas • 8 ounces shredded Cheddar Jack or Mexican cheese blend • 3 plum tomatoes, diced
- 1/2 cup minced onion • salsa, green or tomato, for serving • optional
garnishes: sour cream, sliced green onions, shredded cheese, diced tomatoes,
diced avocados, and sliced ripe olives

PREPARATION

1. Combine the chopped chicken and seasoning mix and toss to coat thoroughly.
2. Spread the refried beans over the tortillas, dividing evenly among the 6
tortillas. Top evenly with the seasoned chicken, shredded cheese, chopped
tomatoes, and minced onions. Roll up. Wrap each burrito in foil and arrange in a
4-to 6-quart slow cooker, stacking if necessary. Cover and cook on HIGH for 2
hours.
3. Serve with salsa and your choice of garnishes.
4. Makes 6 chicken burritos.

Chicken Cacciatore

INGREDIENTS

- 1 large onion, sliced thinly • 1 1/2 pounds skinless, boneless chicken breast halves • 2 (6 oz each) cans tomato paste • 8 ounces fresh sliced mushrooms • 1/2 teaspoon salt • 1/4 teaspoon pepper • 2 cloves garlic minced • 1 teaspoon oregano • 1/2 teaspoon basil • 1 bay leaf • 1/4 cup dry white wine • 1/4 cup water

PREPARATION

1. Put sliced onion in bottom of slow cooker; top with chicken breast halves. Combine and stir together remaining ingredients. Spread over chicken. Cover and cook on low 6 to 8 hours, or 3 to 4 hours on high. Serve as a sauce for hot cooked spaghetti or similar pasta.
2. Serves 4.

Chicken Cassoulet With Navy Beans

INGREDIENTS

- 1/2 cup. dry navy beans, cooked according to package directions until tender
- 1 1/2 lb. chicken pieces with skin removed
- 3/4 cup tomato juice or V-8
- 1/2 cup chopped celery
- 1/2 cup sliced carrots
- 1/2 cup chopped onion
- 1 clove garlic, minced
- 1 medium bay leaf
- 1 teaspoon instant beef bouillon granules or base
- 1/2 teaspoon dried basil
- 1/2 teaspoon dried leaf oregano
- 1/2 teaspoon dried leaf sage, crumbled
- 1/4 teaspoon sweet paprika

PREPARATION

1. Cover and chill the cooked beans.
2. In crockpot, combine cold beans, chicken pieces, tomato juice, celery, carrots, onion, garlic, bay leaf, bouillon, basil, oregano, sage and paprika. Cover and cook on LOW for 7 to 9 hours. Remove and discard bay leaf.
3. Serves 4.

Chicken Chili with Hominy

INGREDIENTS

- 2 pounds chicken breasts, boneless and skinless, cut in 1 to 1 1/2-inch pieces • 1 medium onion, chopped • 3 cloves garlic, thinly sliced • 1 can (15 oz) white hominy, drained • 1 can (14 oz) diced tomatoes, undrained
- 1 can (28 oz) tomatillos, drained and chopped • 1 can (4 oz) mild green chiles

PREPARATION

1. Combine all ingredients in slow cooker; stir to blend all ingredients. Cover and cook on low for 7 to 9 hours, or high for 4 to 4 1/2 hours.
2. Serves 4 to 6.

Chicken Chow Mein

INGREDIENTS

- 1 to 2 tablespoons vegetable oil
- 1 1/2 pounds boneless chicken breasts, skin removed, cut in 1-inch cubes
- 4 medium carrots, thinly sliced
- 6 to 8 green onions, sliced, including green
- 1 1/2 cups sliced celery
- 1 cup low sodium chicken broth
- 1 tablespoon granulated sugar
- 1/3 cup light soy sauce
- 1/4 teaspoon crushed red pepper flakes
- 1/4 teaspoon ground ginger
- 1 medium clove garlic, crushed
- 1 can (8 ounces) bean sprouts
- 1 can (8 ounces) water chestnuts, sliced
- 1/4 cup cornstarch
- 1/3 cup water

PREPARATION

1. Heat oil in skillet; brown chicken, stirring to brown all sides. Put chicken pieces in crockpot. Stir in all ingredients except cornstarch and water. Cover and cook on low for 6 to 8 hours.
2. Turn to high. Combine cornstarch and cold water in a small bowl; stir until

mixture is smooth and cornstarch is dissolved. Stir into the slow cooker liquids.

Keeping cover slightly ajar to allow steam to escape, cook on HIGH until

thickened, about 15 to 30 minutes (this step can be done more quickly on the

stovetop over medium heat).

3. Serveover rice or Chinese noodles.

4. Serves 6.

Chicken Cordon Bleu Recipe, Slow Cooker

INGREDIENTS

• 4 boneless chicken breast halves • 1 can (10 1/2 ounces) condensed
golden mushroom soup • 1/2 cup water • 1/4 cup dry white wine • 4
thin slices ham • 4 slices Swiss cheese

PREPARATION

1. Pound chicken breasts between sheets of plastic wrap until thinned and
even in thickness.
2. Place 1 slice each of ham and cheese on each chicken breast half.
3. Roll up and place into bottom of slow cooker/Crock Pot.
4. Combine golden mushroom soup, 1/2 cup water, and 1/4 cup of dry white
wine. Mix well and pour over chicken in slow cooker.
5. Cover and cook on low for 6 to 7 hours.
6. Serve with rice or noodles.

Chicken Delish

INGREDIENTS

- 6 to 8 boneless, skinless chicken breast halves • lemon juice • salt and pepper, to taste • celery salt or seasoned salt, to taste • paprika, to taste
- 1 can cream of celery soup • 1 can cream of mushroom soup • 1/3 cup dry white wine • grated Parmesan cheese, to taste • cooked rice

PREPARATION

1. Rinse chicken; pat dry. Season with lemon juice, salt, pepper, celery salt, and paprika. Place chicken in slow cooker. In medium bowl mix soups with wine. Pour over chicken breasts. Sprinkle with Parmesan cheese. Cover and cook on low for 6 to 8 hours. Serve chicken with sauce over hot cooked rice, and pass the Parmesan cheese.
2. Serves 4 to 6.

Chicken Divan with Broccoli and Noodles

INGREDIENTS

- 3 cups cooked, diced chicken • 2 tablespoons chopped onion
- 1 (10 3/4 oz.) can cream of chicken soup • 1/3 cup mayonnaise • 3 tablespoons flour • 2 celery ribs, sliced • 1 (10 oz.) pkg. frozen broccoli cuts, about 1 1/2 to 2 cups • 1/2 teaspoon curry powder, or to taste • 1 tablespoon lemon juice • 1 pound pasta or noodles

PREPARATION

1. In medium bowl, combine all ingredients except noodles. Stir to blend ingredients thoroughly.
2. Spoon the mixture into a lightly buttered slow cooker.
3. Cover and cook on LOW 5 to 7 hours or on HIGH 2 1/2 to 3 1/2 hours.
4. When the chicken and broccoli mixture is nearly done, cook the pasta in boiling salted water following package directions.
5. Serve over hot buttered noodles or pasta.
6. This recipe can be doubled.
7. If too thick, add a little chicken broth.

Chicken Enchiladas for the Slow Cooker

INGREDIENTS

- 1 pkg. chicken breasts (1 - 1 1/2 lbs) • 1 jar chicken gravy • 1 4 oz can
green chiles, chopped • 1 onion, chopped • corn tortillas • shredded
cheese

PREPARATION

1. Combine chicken, gravy, green chiles, and chopped onion in slow cooker;
cover and cook on LOW for 5 to 6 hours. Take chicken out of sauce and shred.
Fill corn tortillas with chicken and sauce. Top with shredded cheese and roll.
Place in baking dish. Pour excess sauce over and sprinkle with more shredded
cheese. Bake at 350° for approximately 15 to 20 minutes.
2. Serves 4 to 6.

Chicken Las Vegas

INGREDIENTS

- 6 boneless chicken breast halves, without skin • 1 can cream of
mushroom soup • 1/2 pint. sour cream • 1 (6 oz.) jar dried, chipped beef

PREPARATION

1. Mix together soup, sour cream and dried beef. Roll chicken in the mixture,
coating well; place in crockpot. Pour remaining mixture over chicken. Cover and
cook on LOW for 5 to 7 hours, until chicken is tender but not dried out. Serve
with hot cooked rice or noodles.
2. Serves 6.

Chicken Lasagna

INGREDIENTS

- 2 large chicken breast halves, boneless
- 2 ribs celery chopped
- 1 small onion, chopped, or 1 to 2 tablespoons dried minced onion
- 1/2 teaspoon thyme
- salt and pepper to taste
- 6 to 9 lasagna noodles
- 1 package frozen spinach, thawed and squeezed dry
- 6 ounces fresh mushrooms, thickly sliced, or 1 4 to 8 ounce can
- 1 1/2 cups shredded Cheddar and American cheese mixture
- 1 can "light" cream of mushroom soup
- 1 can tomatoes with green chiles
- 1 package (1 ounce) dry chicken gravy mix
- 3/4 cup reserved broth

PREPARATION

1. In a 2-quart saucepan, simmer chicken breasts with celery, onion, thyme, salt, and pepper until tender, about 25 minutes. Remove chicken and let cool; cut in bite-size pieces or shred. Reserve 3/4 cup of broth. Discard remaining broth or freeze to use in another recipe. Break lasagna noodles in half; boil for about 5 to

8 minutes, until just a little flexible. Drain and rinse with cold water for easier handling.

2. In a medium bowl, combine soup, tomatoes, gravy mix, and reserved broth. In a 3 1/2 to 4-quart slow cooker/Crock Pot, pour in 3/4 cup of the soup mixture. Place 4 to 6 lasagna noodle halves on top of the soup mixture. Add 1/3 of the spinach, 1/3 of the chicken, 1/3 of the mushrooms, and 1/2 cup of shredded cheese. Pour another 3/4 cup soup mixture over all. Repeat layers 2 more times, ending with remaining soup mixture. Cover and cook on low for 4 to 5 hours. If cooked too long, the noodles might become mushy, so check after about 4 1/2 hours.

3. Serves 4.

Chicken Marengo

INGREDIENTS

- 3 to 4 pounds Chicken parts or boneless breasts • 2 fresh tomatoes,
quartered, or use canned diced tomatoes (14.5 ounces) • 8 ounces fresh
mushrooms • 1 envelope spaghetti sauce mix (about 1 1/2 oz.) •
1/2 cup
dry white wine

PREPARATION

1. Place chicken in bottom of Crock Pot. Top with tomatoes and mushrooms.
Combine dry spaghetti sauce mix with wine and pour over chicken. Cover and
cook on LOW 6 to 8 hours or until chicken is tender (boneless chicken breasts
will be tough if cooked too long).

Chicken Parisienne

INGREDIENTS

- 6 to 8 chicken breast halves • salt, pepper, and paprika • 1/2 cup dry white wine • 1 (10 1/2 oz.) can cream of mushroom soup • 8 ounces sliced mushrooms • 1 cup sour cream • 1/4 cup flour

PREPARATION

1. Sprinkle chicken breasts with salt, pepper and paprika. Place in slow cooker. Mix wine, soup and mushrooms until well combined. Pour over chicken. Sprinkle with paprika. Cover and cook on low for 6 to 8 hours, or until chicken is tender but not too dry. Mix sour cream and flour together; add to the Crock Pot. Cook for about 20 minutes longer, until heated through.
2. Serve with rice or noodles.
3. Serves 6 to 8.

Chicken Parmesan

INGREDIENTS

- 2 tablespoons vegetable oil • 6 to 8 boneless chicken breast halves
- salt, pepper and Italian seasoning • 2 cups spaghetti sauce • 1 bay leaf
- garlic (clove or powder) • 1 cup shredded Mozzarella cheese
- Parmesan cheese, grated • rice or noodles

PREPARATION

1. Heat oil in a skillet over medium heat. Brown chicken with a sprinkling of
salt, pepper and Italian seasoning.
2. Mix spaghetti sauce, bay leaf and garlic in crockpot. Put chicken in the
sauce and cook on LOW for 5 to 6 hours, or until the chicken is cooked through
and tender.
3. Remove chicken and sauce to casserole dish. Sprinkle with mozzarella and
Parmesan cheese. Heat in 350° oven until bubbly and cheese is melted.
4. Serve chicken with sauce over pasta, spaghetti squash, or rice.

Chicken Ragout

INGREDIENTS

- 2 tablespoons vegetable oil • 1/2 cup chopped onion • 3 to 4 pounds chicken parts • 2 tablespoons chopped fresh parsley • 1 1/2 cups chicken broth • 2 potatoes, peeled and diced • 1/4 cup fresh lemon juice • 1 egg, beaten • 2 tablespoons chopped fresh dill

PREPARATION

1. Heat oil in a skillet; brown chicken pieces. Add onion to skillet and cook until onion is tender. Put potatoes in the bottom of the crockpot; place browned chicken and onion on top. Add parsley and 1 1/2 cups chicken broth; cover and cook on LOW for 6 to 8 hours. When ready to serve, stir in lemon juice. Transfer juices to a saucepan. To beaten egg, add half of the hot juices; pour egg mixture into the rest of the juices in saucepan.
2. Cook over low heat, stirring constantly, until thickened. Do not boil. Stir in fresh dill. Arrange hot chicken pieces on a serving platter and pour thickened sauce over chicken.
3. Serves 4 to 6.

Chicken Reuben Casserole

INGREDIENTS

- 32 ounces sauerkraut (jar or bag), rinsed and drained
- 1 cup Russian dressing
- 4 to 6 boneless chicken breast halves, skin removed
- 1 tablespoon prepared mustard
- 1 cup shredded Swiss cheese or Monterey Jack

PREPARATION

1. Layer half of the sauerkraut in the bottom of the pot. Pour 1/3 cup dressing over it; place 2 to 3 chicken breasts on top and spread the mustard on chicken. Top with the remaining sauerkraut and chicken breasts; pour another 1/3 cup of dressing over all and reserve the remaining 1/3 cup of dressing for serving.
2. Cover and cook on low for about 4 hours, or until chicken is cooked through and tender. Sprinkle Swiss cheese and cook until cheese is melted.
3. Serve with reserved dressing.
4. Serves 4 to 6.

Chicken Rice Casserole with Green Beans

INGREDIENTS

- 1 cup uncooked rice, converted (Uncle Ben's) • 2 boneless chicken
breasts • 1 can cream of chicken soup • 1 can cream of mushroom soup
- 2 soup cans water (or part white wine, or sherry) • 1 package dry onion
soup mix • 1/2 teaspoon paprika • .
- Suggested Vegetables: • 1 large carrot, sliced into pennies, optional
- 1 cup of fresh or frozen cut green beans, optional • 1 medium green bell
pepper, chopped, optional • 1 can of corn, drained, optional

PREPARATION

1. Place rice in bottom of crockpot. Pour water over rice. Mix canned soups
and dry soup mix in a bowl, pour over top of rice. Add chopped veggies, your
favorites. Place chicken on top. Sprinkle with paprika. Cook on LOW for 4 1/2
to 6 1/2 hours.
2. Shared by Ness W.

Chicken Thighs, Tex-Mex Style

INGREDIENTS

- 1 to 1 1/2 pounds boneless chicken thighs • 1 can (12 to 15 ounces) whole kernel corn, drained • 1 can (15 ounces) black beans, drained • 1 can (4 ounces) mild chopped green chile pepper • 1 cup chunky salsa • 1 tablespoon taco seasoning • 1/4 teaspoon ground black pepper

PREPARATION

1. Remove excess fat from the chicken thighs and put them in the slow cooker along with the corn, beans, chile peppers, salsa, taco seasoning, and pepper. Stir to blend ingredients. Cover and cook on LOW for 5 1/2 to 6 1/2 hours, or until chicken is tender. Serves 4.

Chicken with Artichokes

INGREDIENTS

- 2 (1 oz) pkgs Bearnaise sauce mix • 1/2 cup dry white wine • 1/2 tsp
tarragon • 1/2 tsp garlic powder • 3 green onions, chopped • 8 ounces
cooked ham, diced • 1 red bell pepper, chopped • 1 pound red potatoes,
scrubbed, cut in 1/2-inch cubes • 1 (9-oz) pkg frozen artichoke halves and
quarters, thawed • 1 pound boneless chicken breasts or chicken tenderloins,
cut in chunks

PREPARATION

1. In a slow cooker, mix both packages of bearnaise sauce mix, wine,
tarragon, and garlic powder until well blended. Add green onions, ham, red
pepper, potatoes, artichokes and chicken. Stir gently. Cover, set heat on low
setting, and cook for 6 hours.
2. Serves 4 to 6

Chicken with Bacon and Macaroni

INGREDIENTS

- vegetable oil, about 2 tablespoons • 4 to 6 chicken breast halves, or use 3
pounds chicken parts • 6 slices of bacon • 1/2 cup chopped onion • salt
and pepper • 1/2 teaspoon freshly ground pepper • 1/4 cup chicken broth
- 8 ounces elbow macaroni or small shells, cooked • 2 teaspoons dried
parsley flakes, crumbled

PREPARATION

1. Brown chicken, a few pieces at a time in oil and drain Fry bacon lightly in
the same pan, remove, set aside and pour off all fat. Place chicken and bacon in
slow cooker; add onion, salt, pepper and broth. Cover and cook on low 7 to 8
hours, high 3 to 4 hours, or until chicken is tender. Turn to high, add hot cooked
macaroni and parsley flakes. Cook 15 minutes longer; taste and adjust
seasonings if necessary.

Chicken With Bacon and Wine

INGREDIENTS

- 4 to 5 chicken breasts & thighs • 8 bacon slices, diced • 1 1/2 cups
sliced green onions • 8 small white onions peeled • 16 small new potatoes,
scrubbed, or 1 to 1 1/2 pounds • medium potatoes, quartered • 8 ounces
small whole mushrooms • 3 cloves garlic, crushed and minced
- 2 tsp. salt
- 1/4 tsp. pepper • 1 tsp. dried thyme leaves • 1 cup chicken broth • 1
cup dry red wine • chopped parsley, for garnish • 1 to 2 tablespoons each,
water and flour, optional

PREPARATION

1. In large skillet, sauté diced bacon and green onions until bacon is crisp.
Remove and drain on paper towels. Add chicken pieces to skillet and brown well
on all sides. Remove browned chicken and set aside. Put onions, potatoes,
mushrooms and garlic in crockpot. Add browned chicken pieces, bacon, green
onions, salt, pepper, thyme, and chicken broth. Cover and cook on LOW for 6 to
8 hours, or on HIGH for 3 to 4 hours.

2. Add the wine about 1 hour before done. Remove chicken pieces to serving
platter. If desired, thicken juices with a combination of 1 to 2 tablespoons each
flour and cold water. Arrange vegetables around chicken and pour juices over
all. Garnish with chopped parsley.

Chicken With Biscuits

INGREDIENTS

- 1 1/2 to 2 pounds boneless chicken breast halves, cut in large chunks
- 1/2 cup chopped onion
- 1 cup chopped celery
- 1 can (10 3/4 ounces) condensed cream of chicken or cream of chicken and mushroom soup, undiluted
- 1 jar (12 ounces) chicken gravy
- 1/4 teaspoon poultry seasoning
- 1/2 teaspoon dried leaf thyme
- Dash black pepper
- 2 cups frozen mixed vegetables, thawed
- 6 frozen biscuits or refrigerator biscuits

PREPARATION

1. In a slow cooker, layer the chunks of uncooked chicken breasts with chopped onion and celery.
2. Combine the soup and gravy with poultry seasoning, thyme, and pepper; pour over the chicken.
3. Cover and cook on LOW for 5 to 6 hours.
4. Add the thawed mixed vegetables, turn the slow cooker to HIGH, and continue cooking for 20 to 30 minutes, until vegetables are tender.
5. Meanwhile, bake the biscuits as directed on the package.

1. To serve, split a biscuit and spoon some of the chicken and vegetables over
the bottom half. Put the top half of the biscuit on the chicken and gravy.Serves 6.

Chicken with Cranberries

INGREDIENTS

- 6 boneless, skinless chicken breasts • 1 small onion, chopped
- 1 cup fresh cranberries • 1 teaspoon salt • 1/4 teaspoon ground cinnamon
- 1/4 teaspoon ground ginger • 3 tablespoons brown sugar or honey • 1 cup orange juice • 3 tablespoons flour mixed with 2 tablespoons cold water

PREPARATION

1. Place all ingredients, except flour and water mixture, in the slow cooker or Crock Pot. Cover and cook on low 6 to 7 hours, until chicken is tender. Add flour mixture in the last 15 to 20 minutes and cook until thickened. Taste and adjust seasonings.
2. Serves 4.

Chicken with Dried Beef

INGREDIENTS

- 1 jar dried beef, about 2 1/2 ounces, rinsed • 6 boneless chicken breast halves, skin removed • 6 slices bacon • 1/4 cup sour cream • 1/4 cup flour • 1 can cream of mushroom soup, undiluted • 2 to 3 tablespoons dry white wine, optional

PREPARATION

1. On bottom of greased slow cooke, arrange dried beef. Wrap each piece of chicken with a strip of bacon; arrange on top of dried beef. In small bowl, combine sour cream and flour; add soup and wine, if using, and blend thoroughly. Pour over chicken mixture. Cover and cook on LOW for 6 to 8 hours.
2. Serves 6.
3. Serve with hot cooked rice and salad or potatoes and a green vegetable.

Chicken With Garlic and Pineapple

INGREDIENTS

- 3 1/2 pounds chicken • salt • pepper • 1/4 teaspoon ground ginger
- 1 clove garlic, minced • 1 cup chicken broth • 8 1/2 ounces pineapple,
sliced in syrup, reserve syrup • 4 ounces sliced water chestnuts, drained • 4
green onions, thinly sliced • 1/4 cup cornstarch • 1/4 cup soy sauce • 1
tablespoon vinegar

PREPARATION

1. Sprinkle chicken with salt and pepper; place in slow cooker. Combine
ginger, garlic, chicken broth, and syrup from pineapple; set aside. Cut pineapple
slices into quarters. Arrange pineapple and sliced water chestnuts over chicken.
Pour garlic ginger sauce over all. Cover and cook on HIGH 1 hour; reduce heat
to low and cook an additional 3 to 5 hours or until chicken is tender. Add green
onions. Dissolve cornstarch in soy sauce and vinegar then stir into crockpot.
2. Cover and cook on HIGH 10 to 15 minutes longer, or until slightly thickened.
3. Serve with hot cooked rice.

Chicken with Grapes

INGREDIENTS

- 4 to 6 boneless, skinless chicken breast halves
- 1 tablespoon butter
- 2 tablespoons lemon juice
- 1 tablespoon dry sherry or white wine
- 8 to 12 ounces fresh mushrooms sliced
- salt and pepper to taste
- 1 tablespoon cornstarch mixed with 1 tablespoon water
- 1 cup green seedless grapes

PREPARATION

1. Place chicken, butter, lemon juice, sherry, mushrooms, and salt and pepper in the slow cooker/Crock Pot. Cover and cook on low for 6 to 8 hours. Stir in the cornstarch mixture and grapes during the last 45 minutes. (May be cooked on high 3 1/2 to 4 1/2 hours, adding grapes the last 20 minutes. Serve over rice.
2. Serves 4 to 6.

Chicken With Honey

INGREDIENTS

- 3 to 4 pounds chicken pieces • salt, pepper, and garlic powder
- 1/2 cup soy sauce • 1/2 cup water • 1/2 cup green onion, chopped • 1/2 cup honey

PREPARATION

1. Sprinkle chicken with salt, pepper, and a little garlic powder; place in slow cooker. Combine water, soy sauce, and chopped onion and pour over chicken.
Cover and cook on LOW 3-4 hours or until chicken is render. Remove chicken from pot. Arrange on broiler pan and brush honey on chicken. Broil until golden brown, brushing with honey several times.
2. Serves 4.

Chicken with Macaroni and Smoked Gouda Cheese

INGREDIENTS

- 1 1/2 pounds chicken tenders, boneless • 2 small zucchini, halved and
sliced 1/8-inch thick • 1 package chicken gravy mix (approx. 1 oz) • 2
tablespoons water • salt and pepper to taste • pinch of ground nutmeg,
fresh if possible • 8 ounces smoked Gouda cheese, grated • 2 tablespoons
evaporated milk or light cream • 1 large tomato, chopped • 4 cups cooked
macaroni or small shell pasta

PREPARATION

1. Cut chicken into 1-inch cubes; place in crockpot. Add zucchini, gravy mix,
water, and seasoning. Cover and cook for 5 to 6 hours on low. Add smoked
gouda cheese, milk or cream, and chopped tomato to the crockpot during the last
20 minutes, or while the macaroni is cooking. Stir in hot cooked macaroni.
2. Chicken recipe serves 4.

Chicken With Noodles, Slow Cooker

INGREDIENTS

- 2 teaspoons chicken bouillon granules or base • 1 tablespoon chopped
fresh parsley • 3/4 teaspoon poultry seasoning • 1/3 cup. diced Canadian
bacon or smoked ham • 2 to 3 carrots, thinly sliced • 2 ribs celery, thinly
sliced • 1 small onion, thinly sliced • 1/4 cup. water • 1 broiler-fryer
chicken (about 3 pounds), cut up • 1 (10 3/4 oz.) can condensed cheddar
cheese soup • 1 tablespoon all purpose flour • 1 (16 oz.) pkg. wide egg
noodles, cooked and drained • 2 tablespoons sliced pimento • 2
tablespoons grated Parmesan cheese

PREPARATION

1. In a small bowl, combine chicken bouillon or base, chopped parsley, and
poultry seasoning; set aside.
2. In slow cooker, layer Canadian bacon or ham, carrots, celery and onion.
Add water.
3. Remove skin and excess fat from chicken; rinse and pat dry. Place half the

chicken in slow cooker. Sprinkle with half of the reserved seasoning mixture.

Top with remaining chicken and sprinkle with remaining seasoning mixture.

4. Stir soup and flour together and spoon over the chicken; do not stir.

5. Cover and cook on HIGH for 3 to 3 1/2 hours or on low for 6 to 8 hours, or

until chicken is tender and juices from chicken run clear when cut along the bone

and vegetables are tender.

6. Put hot cooked noodles in a shallow 2 to 2 1/2 quart broiler proof serving

dish. Arrange chicken over the noodles. Stir soup mixture and vegetables in

crockpot until blended. Spoon vegetables and some of the liquid over chicken.

Sprinkle with sliced pimiento and Parmesan cheese.

7. Broil 4 to 6 inches from heat source for 5 to 8 minutes, or until lightly

browned.

8. Garnish with parsley sprig if desired.

9. Alpine chicken recipe serves 4 to 6.

Chicken with Onions

INGREDIENTS

- 4 large onions, sliced thinly • 5 cloves garlic, minced • 1/4 cup lemon juice • 1 teaspoon salt • 1/4 teaspoon cayenne pepper (or more if you like)
- 4 to 6 frozen boneless chicken breasts, no need to thaw • hot cooked rice

PREPARATION

1. Put all ingredients except rice in Crock Pot. Mix well. Cook for 4 to 6 hours on LOW, or until chicken is cooked through and still tender.
2. Serve over rice.

Chicken With Parsley Dumplings

INGREDIENTS

- 4 to 6 chicken breast halves, skin removed • 1 dash each salt, pepper,
dried leaf thyme, ground marjoram and paprika • 1 large onion, sliced,
divided • 2 leeks, sliced • 4 carrots, cut large chunks • 1 garlic clove,
minced • 1 cup chicken broth • 1 tablespoon cornstarch • 1 can (10 3/4
ounces) condensed cream of chicken soup • 1/2 cup dry white wine
- Dumplings • 1 cup Bisquick • 8 tablespoons milk • 1 teaspoon dried parsley flakes • dash salt • dash pepper • dash paprika

PREPARATION

1. Sprinkle salt, pepper, thyme, marjoram, and paprika on chicken. In bottom
of crockpot, place half of the onion slices, leeks, and carrots. Arrange chicken on
vegetables. Sprinkle minced garlic over the chicken then top with remaining
onion slices. Dissolve 1 tablespoon cornstarch in 1 cup of chicken broth then
combine with the cream of chicken soup and wine. Cook on HIGH for about 3
hours or on LOW for about 6 hours (If cooking on LOW, turn to HIGH when

dumplings are added).
2. Chicken should be tender, but not dry.
3. Dumplings: Mix together 1 cup bisquick, about 8 tablespoon milk,
parsley, salt, pepper, and paprika; form into balls and place on top of the chicken
mixture the last 35 to 45 minutes of cooking.
4. Serves 4 to 6.

Chicken With Pearl Onions and Mushrooms

INGREDIENTS

- 4 to 6 boneless chicken breast halves, cut in 1-inch chunks
- 1 can (10 3/4 ounces) cream of chicken or cream of chicken and mushroom soup
- 8 ounces sliced mushrooms
- 1 bag (16 ounces) frozen pearl onions
- salt and pepper, to taste
- parsley, chopped, for garnish

PREPARATION

1. Wash chicken and pat dry. Cut into chunks about 1/2 to 1-inch and put in a large bowl. Add the soup, mushrooms, and onions; stir to combine. Spray the slow cooker insert with cooking spray.
2. Spoon the chicken mixture into the crockpot and sprinkle with salt and pepper.
3. Cover and cook on LOW for 6 to 8 hours, stirring about halfway through the cooking time, if possible.
4. Garnish with fresh chopped parsley, if desired, and serve over hot cooked rice or with potatoes.
5. Serves 4 to 6.

Conclusion

Thank you again for purchasing this book!
I hope this book was able to help you discover some amazing Crock Pot Recipes. The next step is to get cooking!!!

www.ingramcontent.com/pod-product-compliance
Lightning Source LLC
Chambersburg PA
CBHW070914080526
44589CB00013B/1286